LAS VEGAS

IN PHOTOGRAPHS

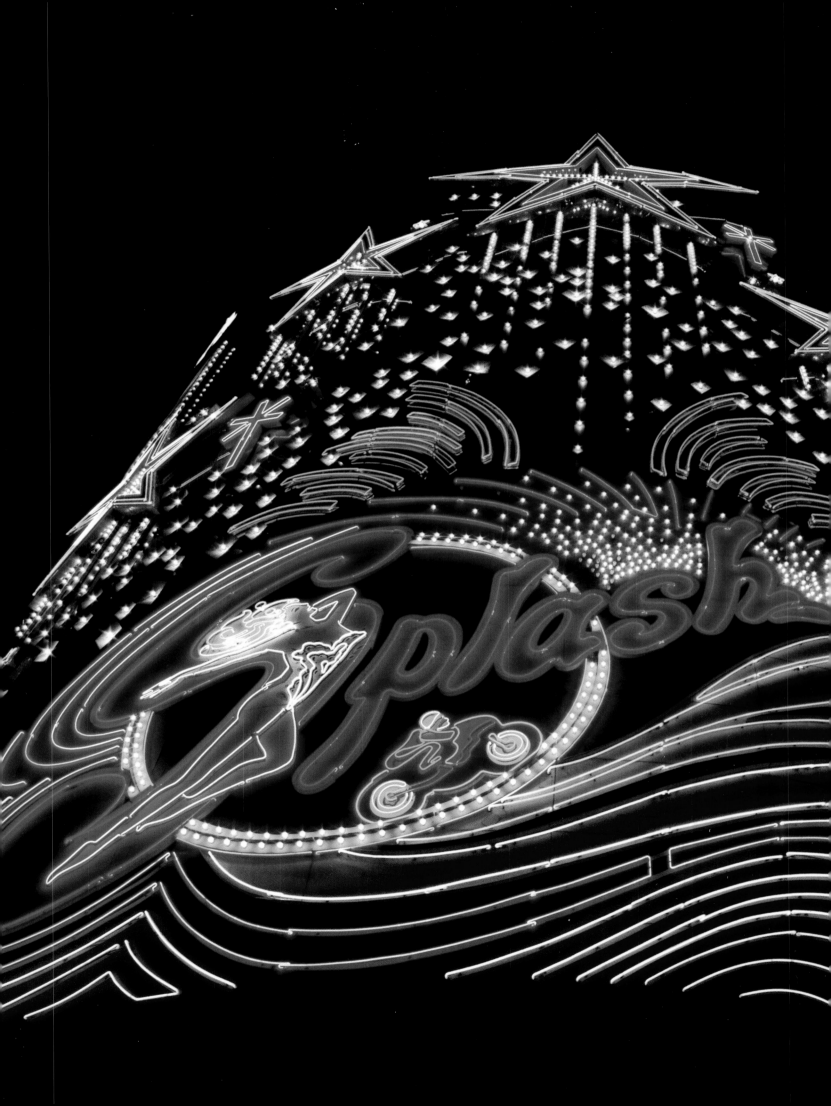

LAS VEGAS

IN PHOTOGRAPHS

SCOTT THARLER

GRAMERCY BOOKS
NEW YORK

© 2006 Salamander Books
An imprint of Anova Books Company Ltd
151 Freston Road, London, W10 6TH

Published by Gramercy Books,
an imprint of Random House Value Publishing,
a division of Random House, Inc., New York,
by arrangement with Anova Books, London.

Gramercy is a registered trademark and the
colophon is a trademark of Random House, Inc.

Random House
New York • Toronto • London • Sydney • Auckland
www.randomhouse.com

Printed and bound in China

A catalog record for this title is available from the Library
of Congress.

ISBN-13: 978-0-517-22875-3
ISBN-10: 0-517-22875-0

10 9 8 7 6 5 4 3 2 1

Credits
Editor: Martin Howard
Designer: Cara Rogers
Production: Kate Rogers
Reproduction: Anorax Imaging Ltd

Additional captions

Acknowledgments
For being a great companion on our various trips to Vegas, Lisa
Stacy Amer. I would also like to thank photogapher Barrett Adams
who shot the substantial proportion of photographs in the book,
Deanna DeMatteo's helpful and thorough web site
lvstriphistory.com and John A. Piet, Senior Research Analyst for the
Las Vegas Convention and Visitors Authority.

Picture Acknowledgments
All images © Barrett Adams/Anova Image Library except for the
following:

© ALAMY: © Imagestate/Alamy: p25; © D. Hurst/Alamy p28.
© CORBIS: © Richard Cummins/Corbis: p13; © Rachel Royse/
Corbis: p38; © Erik Perel/IconSMI/Corbis: p116.
© Mandalay Bay Resort & Casino, Las Vegas: p73.
© MGM Mirage: p7, p10, p46, p48, p49, p57, p60, p78, p79, p80,
p81, p82, p84.
© Sahara Hotel & Casino, Las Vegas: p31, p32, p33.
© Superstock/Richard Cummins: p45.

Contents

INTRODUCTION

Las Vegas' legendary pioneers left us a story as colorful and vibrant as any glossy photograph. Runaway farmworkers, spirited trailblazers, ambitious missionaries, scheming politicians, mobsters, and visionary businessmen are among those who pitted their wits against the surrounding Mojave Desert to build the world's most unique and exciting city. The metropolis has grown to be not only a glorious gambling and entertainment mecca, but also the largest U.S. city founded in the twentieth century.

Las Vegas owes its existence to the thing that is most precious in the desert: water. The city is literally an oasis. Before it was host to some of the biggest, most glittering hotels in the world, Spanish explorers and traders found a verdant meadow, which they named Las Vegas, which means "the meadows" in Spanish.

The most famous story of Las Vegas' discovery tells that in late 1829, New Mexican merchant Antonio Armijo was leading the first commercial caravan to follow a portion of the Old Spanish Trail. On Christmas Day, as the large party of sixty traders camped on the Virgin River a hundred miles northeast of present day Las Vegas, Armijo sent ahead a reconnaissance team. Most of the scouts returned a week later, but one of them didn't rejoin the group until the following week. As the widely celebrated legend goes, teenager Rafael Rivera had ventured off on his own, spotted artesian springs and a fertile green plain in the middle of the desert, and named the area. Unfortunately, modern historians, among them Frank Wright (1938–2003), well-respected author and former curator for the Nevada State Museum and Historical Society, have recently discovered evidence that does not support the story about Rivera. Instead, as Wright suggests, "It was some later, and as yet unidentified, party that would happen upon the springs and record the place as 'The Meadows' on Mexican maps."

Although Rivera does not appear to have been the first person of European ancestry to enter the lush Las Vegas Valley, when the desert oasis was eventually discovered in the 1830s, it provided a welcome shortcut and necessary stopover for weary travelers. One such traveler was Captain John C. Fremont, who led a large scientific surveying expedition that camped at Las Vegas Springs on May 3, 1844. The group—which included heroic scout Kit Carson, for whom Nevada's capital would later be named—had been commissioned by the U.S. Army Corps of Engineers. Fremont meticulously mapped and wrote about the area, and then journeyed north to Salt Lake City.

Fremont's work had a significant impact on the history of Las Vegas, which is no doubt why the main Downtown drag is named after him. First, his maps aided the U.S. Army in its invasion of Mexico, which several years later had huge geographic ramifications. By 1848, Mexico was officially forced to cede nearly half its territory, which would become the states of Texas, Colorado, Utah, Arizona, New Mexico, California, and Nevada. And second, Fremont's widely published journals brought the valley to the widespread attention of popular culture. Many would utilize the information Fremont disseminated, including Las Vegas' first official (non-Native American) settlers.

In May 1855, after annexation by the United States, Brigham Young assigned thirty Mormons, led by William Bringhurst, to establish the Las Vegas Mission. The colonists used Fremont's route (in reverse) to get from Salt Lake City to Las Vegas.

▶ **New York–New York:** *In January 1997, New York–New York opened at the intersection of Tropicana and Las Vegas Boulevards. Seen outdoors is the half-scale Statue of Liberty, Brooklyn Bridge replica, and skyline-defining Empire State and Chrysler buildings; the Big Apple theme continues indoors with homages to Central Park and Greenwich Village.*

There they aimed to convert the native Southern Paiutes—who had dwelled in nearby campsites for hundreds of years—by teaching them farming techniques. The missionaries built a 150-square-foot adobe fort (the oldest structure in Las Vegas, part of which still survives today as a registered national historic site). It would serve as a safe haven for travelers—including mail carriers on the newly established monthly U.S. postal delivery route—along the Salt Lake City to Los Angeles, which was known as the "Mormon Corridor." For two years, the settlers struggled among themselves, with Native raids, and against the harsh desert environment. Eventually they abandoned the fort in 1857.

Nevada officially adopted its name (Spanish for "snow-covered") in 1861, and "The Battle-Born State" became the thirty-sixth member of the United States, strategically added to the Union during the Civil War in 1864. The following year, Arizona legislator Octavius Decatur Gass took over the Mormon fort and turned the area into a ranch, winery, and farming operation.

Although the ranch grew over the next dozen years, O.D. Gass slid deep into debt, eventually defaulting on a personal $5,000 loan from Archibald Stewart. As the new owner, Stewart expanded the ranch to more than 1,800 acres and began to make it profitable. But under suspicious circumstances in July 1884, Archibald Stewart was murdered. His wife Helen continued to run the farm successfully through to the end of the century. During that time, the state sold much of its land (at $1.25 per acre!), the area's agriculture flourished, and the discovery of lead and silver led to mining nearby.

In 1902, Helen Stewart sold all of her 1,840 acres—except the family cemetery and a small section of Las Vegas creek—to the notoriously corrupt railroad tycoon and Montana Senator William A. Clark. Meanwhile, also seeing the opportunity to strike it rich during the impending boom, surveyor James T. McWilliams snatched up an unclaimed

◀ **Treasure Island:** At the forefront of high-impact production shows, Treasure Island landed Mystère, the first of several resident Cirque du Soleil shows in Las Vegas. Its Sirens of TI blends singing, dancing, and pyrotechnics in the only free outdoor show with live performers on the Strip.

acreage of the former Stewart farm. McWilliams sold cheap lots to miners, gamblers, and cowboys. Over the next couple of years, thousands flocked to the tent town that had now sprouted a post office, a hotel, banks, restaurants, markets, and a glut of saloons and gambling halls. In 1904, Clark's San Pedro, Los Angeles & Salt Lake City Railroad—later absorbed by Union Pacific—linked the railway from Utah to southern California. Las Vegas became an important refueling point and rest stop. Superseding McWilliams' concurrent attempt at a township, Clark's railroad successfully laid out a town and held a two-day site auction. On May 15, 1905, the 110 acres now bound by Stewart Avenue (north), Garces Avenue (south), Main Street (west) and Fifth Street (east) were sold. The dusty little railroad town of Las Vegas was officially born.

In its infancy the frontier town was centered around the railroad—its connection to civilization—as well as the infamous Block 16, the town's red light district. Surviving photographs show what must have been an isolated place to live, with tumbleweed blowing along dirt streets. Nevertheless, over the following decades the little town continued to grow, the streets became paved and civic buildings such as schools and courthouses—the marks of permanence—appeared, along with more and bigger houses. But it was the construction of the Hoover Dam (originally named the Boulder Dam), rather than the railroad, that sparked Las Vegas' real boom.

During the dam's construction, which lasted from 1931 to 1935, thousands of workers and their families flooded into the area. Most of them settled at Boulder City, which was specially constructed to house them. That town, however, was run on strict Christian principles, whereas Las Vegas had just repealed its ban on gambling. The result was an influx of workers looking for a good time, with ready money to spend. The newly built gambling halls and hotels on Fremont Street did a roaring trade and the city's fame began to spread, attracting tourists from further afield.

With so much wealth to be had, businesses soon began to vie with each other for the most profit, and the newly discovered neon began to appear. Then in the forties came the most dramatic development of all: along the previously deserted Highway 91,

enterprising businessmen began to build the first resort/hotel/casinos. The Strip was born. The El Rancho was first, but its success saw others follow suit quickly. With the completion of Benjamin "Bugsy" Siegel's Flamingo, the mob also moved into Las Vegas.

The fifties saw the Strip becoming even grander, leaving Downtown lagging. The Desert Inn, Sahara, Sands, Riviera, and Dunes were all completed during this time. With so much competition, the new resorts needed more than just stunning lightshows to attract customers, and the fifties also saw the beginning of another Las Vegas staple—entertainment spectacles. Shows like *Folies Bergère*, which included feathered and jeweled showgirls, were wildly popular. Eager to fill the gaming halls, atomic blasts at the close-by Nevada Test Site were even promoted by the city as a tourist attraction.

During the sixties and seventies the adult-oriented wonderland grew upward as well as along Las Vegas Boulevard, with high-rise hotels replacing intimate poolside bungalows. In 1966, the mighty Caesars Palace was finished, and changed the face of Las Vegas again. This themed mega-resort set a new benchmark for all the hotel/casinos to follow. Two years later Circus Circus opened its doors, becoming the first family destination in Las Vegas, a trend that would pick up again decades later with Excalibur. It seems that the new generation of Vegas entrepreneurs knew what they were doing: in 1975, Nevada's income from gambling exceeded one billion dollars for the first time.

A city built on such intense competition has little time for its heritage, and some of the grand dames of Las Vegas have now sadly gone. The Sands, for example, once the casino of choice for the Rat Pack, was imploded to make room for Venetian. However, old time Las Vegas can still be found, most notably on Fremont Street, under the technological wizardry of the Fremont Street Experience. And in

◀ **Bellagio:** *Built to capture the elegance of classical Italian architecture, Bellagio is the last word in luxury on the Strip. The resort features a fine art gallery, seasonally themed conservatory, upscale shopping, lake-facing haute cuisine restaurants, and, of course, the famous dancing fountains, one of Las Vegas' most well-known sights.*

terms of offering ever more heady levels of sophistication and excitement, the city goes from strength to strength. More recent additions to the Strip, such as Bellagio, Mandalay Bay, the MGM Grand, Paris, New York-New York, and Luxor are among the most awe-inspiring destinations in the world, and there is always the promise of more to come. After surviving the grandest of financial swings over the last century, Las Vegas is thriving as never before. Synonymous with gaming and nightlife, the ultimate desert oasis seems to always be redefining itself by way of world-class resorts, dining, and entertainment. The caché of flashy megastructures in and around Downtown and the Strip are modern marvels of architecture and engineering, as much as they are hyperbole-defying caricatures. To complete the picture, the natural beauty of the surrounding area's terrain is also visually stunning. Which goes a way in explaining why more than 6,000 people a month move into the city, and why upward of forty million tourists a year visit Las Vegas.

▼ **Wynn, Treasure Island, and Mirage casinos:** *These modern casinos have demonstrated that the future lies with the big new resorts, while the older casinos, such as Westward Ho and the New Frontier, have either closed or been subjected to billion-dollar makeovers.*

Venetian: *In November 1996, The Sands was imploded to make way for Venetian, which opened two and a half years later. With the underground-connected Sands Expo, the addition of the Venezia tower, and 3,025-suite Palazzo extension, Venetian holds the record as the largest resort and hotel complex in the world.*

Bally's and Flamingo: *Right at the heart of the Central Strip on either side of Flamingo Road, Bally's and the Flamingo Hilton embody completely different eras. While the Flamingo conjures images of mobsters and the decadence of the forties and fifties, Bally's exudes a more subtle, modern-but-classic image born in the eighties.*

Downtown

From its early twentieth century beginnings as a vice-filled railroad watering stop to its late twentieth century makeover as a family-oriented entertainment destination, "Glitter Gulch" has certainly seen—and survived—its share of ups and downs.

In 1906, newly installed slot machines enjoyed instant popularity in Vegas shops and saloons such as the notorious Arizona Club on Block 16, the city's bawdy red light district. That same year, Downtown's first hotel, Hotel Nevada (now the Golden Gate Hotel and Casino) opened its doors. Fancy for its time, the two-story hotel offered ten-by-ten foot rooms with electric lighting (but no air conditioning) for a dollar a day.

The next five years had a huge impact in shaping Las Vegas. In 1909, it became the seat of the newly established Clark County. In 1910, a strict law was passed against the gambling that had already been allowed for over forty years, sending that community underground. And in March 1911, Las Vegas officially adopted its charter, becoming an incorporated city.

The hopeful young city faced hard times in the 1920s, with strikes and layoffs affecting its staple industry, the railroad. But while the rest of the country suffered throughout the Great Depression, Las Vegas exploded. As fortune would have it, the city reinstituted legalized gambling in 1931, the same year that tens of thousands of job-seekers flooded the area hoping to earn money on the Boulder Dam Project. Las Vegas issued its first gaming license to the Northern Club in March 1931, and others soon followed. Most of the classic joints on Fremont Street, still recognizable today, such as the Pioneer Club and Golden Nugget, sprang up between the dam's completion in 1936 and the end of the fifties. The forties also saw the seeding of the soon-to-be-world-famous Las Vegas Strip.

After several decades of economic struggles, a cooperative of local hotel-casinos invested millions of dollars to revitalize Downtown. In 1994, almost seventy years after it was first paved, Fremont Street was closed to automobile traffic. And in 1995, the sensory overload of the Fremont Street Experience debuted above a safer, friendlier Fremont pedestrian walkway. Although it may always play second fiddle, taking in only about a tenth as much revenue as the Strip, the Downtown area of Las Vegas is still richer in history.

▶ **Vegas Vic:** *One of the most recognizable Vegas icons, the famous and friendly neon-clad cowboy is forty feet tall. Vic has been standing over the Pioneer Club on Fremont Street since 1950. He underwent a major refurbishing in 2000, but sadly he no longer waves his arm or startles passers by with the occasional "Howdy, pardner, welcome to Las Vegas!" that used to blast from his electronic voicebox.*

▶ **The Golden Nugget:** *The Hand of Faith, found near the Golden Triangle in Australia, is the world's largest known gold nugget. Appropriately, in 1981, the eighteen-inch, sixty-pound metallic chunk was moved and put on display in the lobby of the famous Golden Nugget resort, the largest hotel-casino Downtown.*

◀ **Fremont Street Experience:** *A 12.5 million LED module display fills the barrel vault canopy that stretches five blocks and towers ninety feet (at its peak) over Fremont Street. Every hour from dusk until midnight, dazzling animated light shows dance approximately 1,500 feet across the underside of the curved structure, as music booms through the 540,000-watt sound system.*

▶ **Vegas Vicki:** *The bright, coquettish, boot-sporting vixen was presumably built as a companion of sorts for Vic across the way. Originally named "Sassy Sally" after the strip joint she adorned, which became the Mermaids casino and smoothie bar in 1993, Vicki's leg was planned to kick up and down, but never did.*

◀ **Fremont Street:**
A bewildering display of light
and sound, Fremont Street at
night is a melange of new
technologies and old-style
Vegas. Binion's, for example,
was founded by a Texan
bootlegger. During the sixties
it was the most popular
gambling spot in Vegas.

▲ **Neonopolis:** In 1898,
chemists William Ramsay
and Morris Travers discovered
the inert gas that, when
harnessed, would change
the landscape of Las Vegas
into a wonderland of light.
Neonopolis, on Fremont
Street, celebrates the
bright, glowing, often gaudy,
neon signs that are

synonymous with Sin City.
Tourists can also visit the
nearby Neon Museum's
outdoor "boneyard" to see
original and restored vintage
signs from as early as the
1940s.

▶ **Old Las Vegas
Mormon Fort State
Historic Park:** Remnants
of the monumental adobe
fort mark the first permanent
structure built by non-native
settlers in Las Vegas. In 2000,
143 years after the
Mormons abandoned it, the
fort officially became a state
park open to the public.

Northern Strip

Having owned a string of California motor inns, Thomas Hull decided to open a Western-themed resort on the two-lane U.S. Highway 91, just south of the Las Vegas city limits. That resort, the El Rancho, opened April 3, 1941 with sixty-three rooms. Although it was the first hotel, it wasn't the first casino on what would later be named Las Vegas Boulevard (but which is most commonly referred to as "the Strip"). That distinction had been earned ten years earlier by the Pair-o-Dice Club, which, after the El Rancho's success, was rebuilt and reopened in October 1942 as the Hotel Last Frontier.

For the duration of World War II, Las Vegas resort growth slowed. But at the end of 1946, the fancy Flamingo opened about two miles south of the El Rancho. It featured lavish, Miami-inspired décor that raised the bar for the subsequent properties, starting with such noteworthy Northern Strip casino-hotels as the Sahara, Stardust, and Riviera, which came to life in the fifties.

The fifties also brought political intrigue to Vegas. Senator Estes Kefauver, in a bid to fulfill higher career aspirations, led well-publicized hearings aimed at uncovering suspected crooked casino operations. Businessman Wilbur Clarke testified in November 1950, just seven months after opening the Desert Inn, that a Cleveland-based syndicate headed by bootlegger/racketeer Morris "Moe" Dalitz had backed the property's construction. Apparently, the syndicate had acquired a 75 percent silent ownership of the Desert Inn with a subsidy from the Teamsters' pension fund—a method Dalitz repeated to complete the Stardust in 1955.

In November 1966, billionaire recluse Howard Hughes and his touring entourage rented the entire top floor of the Desert Inn, much to the chagrin of Dalitz. Despite repeatedly asking Hughes to leave to make room for the high rollers, Dalitz met with resistance. Finally, Hughes simply negotiated to buy the resort. Eventually, in March 1967, Hughes assumed seven million dollars in liabilities and paid over six million in cash to Moe Dalitz for the Desert Inn.

Having developed a taste for Vegas properties, Hughes continued snatching up casino-resorts, such as the Sands, Silver Slipper, and New Frontier. To help facilitate the process, Nevada passed special legislation allowing the more "legitimate" publicly traded corporations to obtain gambling licenses, starting in the late sixties. Thus, Howard Hughes was responsible for ushering in the modern age of conglomerate-owned Vegas.

▶ **Circus Circus:** *Presided over by Lucky the Clown, Circus Circus has been welcoming guests since 1968. The resort prides itself on being a destination for the whole family and, as well as the casino, has a massive indoor theme park called Adventuredome, with rollercoasters, funfair rides, and games.*

◀ **Wynn Las Vegas:**
*Steve Wynn built this $2.7
billion ultra-resort and gave it
to his wife as a birthday
present. Originally planned to
be called La Rêve (meaning
"The Dream"), the simple-
yet-imposing, curved, fifty-
story hotel-casino opened
across the Strip from the
Fashion Show Mall in April
2005 as Wynn Las Vegas.*

▲ **Wynn, Ferrari
Dealership:** *In a town of
excess, sometimes a simple
commemorative T-shirt or
pack of cards from the gift
shop is an inadequate
souvenir, particularly if you're
a high roller on a lucky
streak. Fortunately for those
who want to spend some
serious money, the dealership,
tucked away inside Wynn Las
Vegas, sells both Ferraris and
Maseratis.*

◀ **Fashion Show Mall:** *One of the largest enclosed malls in the world, it lives up to its name by providing fashion shows on an eighty-foot long retractable runway and elevated stage. Inside, various levels boast over 250 shops and restaurants. Just outside, the Cloud, a 480-foot-long, 562-ton, UFO-like steel structure, looms more than 100 feet above the sidewalk and provides a multimedia projection surface at night.*

◀ **Circus Circus:** *Jay Sarno originally planned a themed Roman circus to neighbor his Caesars Palace property. Instead, the casino—with no hotel— opened at a different site up the road in October 1968 with a more traditionally themed "circus circus." Now with over 3,700 rooms, Circus Circus is one of the biggest hotels in the world.*

▶ **Sahara:** *Replacing Club Bingo in 1952, the Moroccan-themed Sahara was the sixth resort to open on the Strip, just across the street from the first, the El Rancho. Strategically located just outside the Las Vegas city limits on the east side of Las Vegas Boulevard, it is one of the oldest remaining resorts.*

◀ **Circus Circus, Acrobats:** *Throughout the day, a variety of acrobats and circus performers take center stage to entertain guests and gamblers for free at "the World's Largest Permanent Circus." Circus Circus' five-acre climate-controlled Adventuredome amusement park is fully enclosed within the largest space-frame dome in the United States. Its carnival midway was featured in the 1971 James Bond film Diamonds Are Forever.*

◀ **Sahara, Poolside:**
The pool at Sahara was
surrounded by intimate
bungalows in the past.
However, in order to stay
competitive with the growing
number of mega-resorts, the
bungalows came down and
up went a twenty-six-story
tower addition. However, the
pool remains, as does its
original Moroccan flavor.
While it is not the most
spectacular pool along the
Strip, it is simple and elegant
and remains a favorite.

▲ **Sahara, Speed–
The Ride:** *Starting inside
the NASCAR Café, the
Sahara rollercoaster quickly
propels passengers at up to
3.5 G-forces and seventy
miles per hour through an
underground tunnel and right*
*into a loop. The ride twists
and turns along the Strip,
through the giant Sahara
marquee and up a ninety-
degree incline that reaches
224 feet off the ground,
before reversing direction
and returning back.*

◀ **Turnberry Place:**
The fourth resort on the Strip started as the Thunderbird in September 1948, then became the Silverbird (1977) and then the second El Rancho (1982). Dormant from 1992 to 2000, its buildings were imploded to make way for the four forty-story luxury towers of Turnberry Place. The first tower is seen here, along with partial views of two of the others. This condominium community occupies the lot north of Riviera and south of Sahara.

▶ **Riviera:** *When it opened in April 1955, Riviera became the ninth hotel on the Strip and the first with a high rise (at nine stories). Its glitzy facade celebrates Splash, Riviera's wildly diverse and entertaining variety show. The hotel-casino's interior has been featured in such popular movies as Ocean's Eleven (1960), Casino (1995) and Go (1999).*

◀ **Crazy Girls Statue:**
To the shock and delight of countless passers-by on the Strip, the showgirls of Riviera's long-running musical topless revue, Crazy Girls, are immortalized in a provocative life-size bronze statue just outside the entrance to the casino.

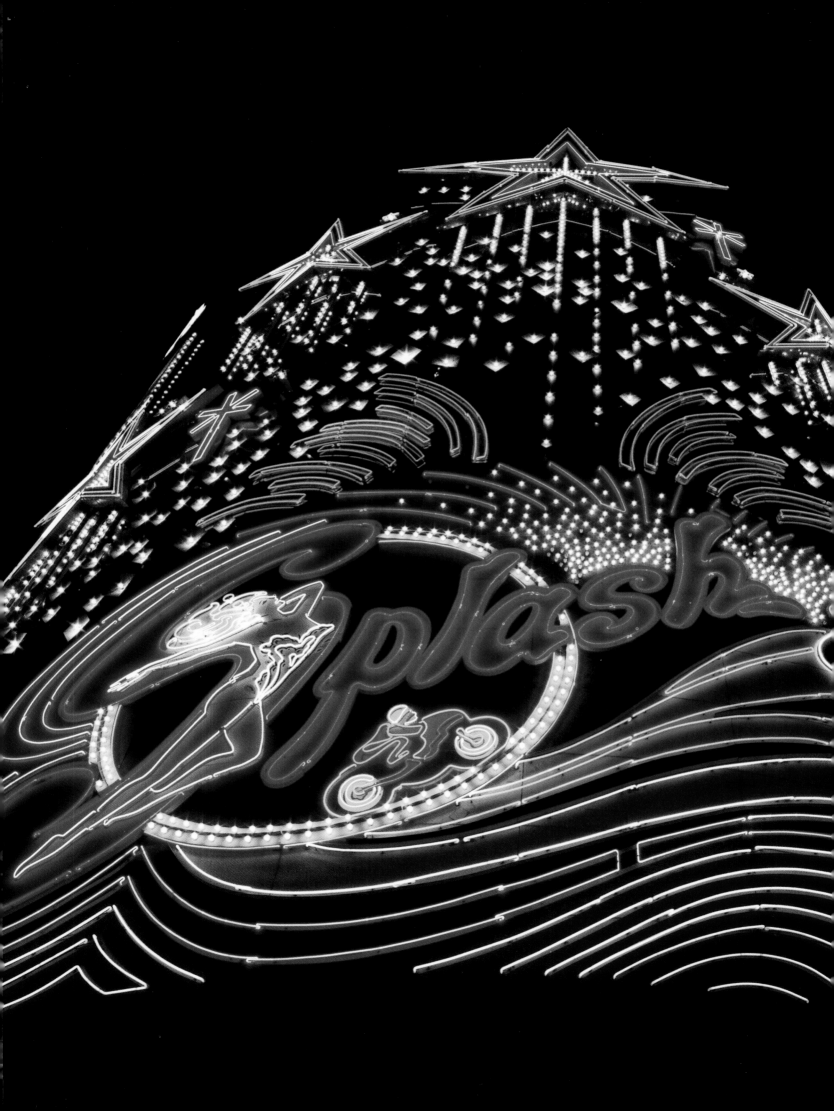

◀ **Stratosphere:** *The Stratosphere observation tower, the biggest in the United States, is easily seen from anywhere in Las Vegas. To lure patrons up to the northernmost resort-casino on the Strip, Stratosphere tends to offer great deals on its hotel rooms and attractive odds on some games—such as single-zero roulette, which cuts the house edge in half.*

▲ **Stratosphere, Thrill Rides:** *Close to the top of the 1,149-foot Stratosphere, the tallest U.S. building west of the Mississippi, are an observation deck, revolving restaurant, and the highest thrill rides in the world. Among them, Insanity and XScream dangle and drop passengers (who have intentionally paid for this experience) over the tower's edge.*

▲ **Stratosphere, View:**
The views of the city and
surrounding Mojave Desert
from the Stratosphere's
observation deck are
outstanding. Guests can see
all the way to the Desert
National Wildlife Range to
the north and over the Strip
to the McCullough Range (as
seen here) to the south.

◀▲ **Wedding Chapels:** *With marriage licenses in hand, affianced couples have many options as to the proper romantic location at which to get hitched. A whole string of variously themed chapels— from traditionally lavish ceremonies to stunningly simple drive-throughs—lines Las Vegas Boulevard north of the Strip on the way to Downtown. The most popular wedding days in Las Vegas are easily Valentine's Day and New Year's Eve. A close second are dates of numerical significance, such as 01/01/01, 02/03/04, or 02/04/06. And finally, helpful for those who may have tied the knot somewhat in haste, Nevada also offers liberal divorces after only six weeks of residency.*

◄ **Stardust:** *The Stardust was the brainchild of Tony Cornero, who died in 1955, before its completion. For decades, it hosted such famous entertainment acts as Lido de Paris, Siegfried and Roy, and Wayne Newton.*

Central Strip

By 1945, reputed gangster Benjamin Siegel—backed by the Meyer Lansky crime organization—had already bought and sold interests in various Vegas casinos. This led Siegel and Lansky to a casino operations innovation: have mobsters invest in, run, and take cash profits from the joint, while the "official" owner known to the public is a respected businessman.

Enter Los Angeles nightclub owner and *Hollywood Reporter* publisher Billy Wilkerson, who originally conceived and began work on the posh Flamingo. After Wilkerson's funds ran dry, he turned the project over to Siegel, who kept Wilkerson as the Flamingo's front man and one-third owner. By the time the upscale Flamingo opened on December 26, 1946, it had cost $6 million—four times the original budget. The East Coast investors (Mafia members) suspected Siegel was on the take. To make matters worse, a slow start caused the Flamingo to temporarily close down.

A month after it reopened in March 1947, Siegel muscled out Wilkerson. But that June, impatient to be repaid, Ben Siegel's business partners murdered him as he sat reading the paper in his girlfriend's Beverly Hills home. Eventually, the lavishly decorated Flamingo, with its wall-to-wall carpeting and other contemporary first-class amenities, attracted plenty of business and made money. Entrepreneurial Benny Siegel's glamorous vision had set the benchmark for Las Vegas resort-casinos' style and elegance. It had also paved the way for the mob-run resorts that came to life throughout the fifties.

In the mid-to-late sixties, the more family-friendly Caesars Palace and Circus Circus opened to relative success. But the mid-seventies were rough for Vegas, between the country's impending energy crisis and the legalization of gaming in newly competitive Atlantic City, New Jersey. Las Vegas was in a serious slump until 1989, the year burgeoning young tycoon Steve Wynn opened the 3,049-room Mirage as a full-blown dining, entertainment, and relaxation destination for the masses. The first "mega-resort" was born.

October 27, 1993 not only marked the opening of The Mirage's neighboring 2,900-room sister property, Treasure Island, but the day Wynn ceremoniously leveled the legendary Dunes. Complete with fireworks and symbolic cannon blasts from Treasure Island's pirate ship, 200,000 anxious onlookers watched the Dunes—which had thirty-six years earlier debuted *Minsky's Follies*, the first topless show—implode to make way for the world's most expensive hotel to date, The Bellagio. Old Vegas was out. The new Vegas, which would grow to house seventeen of the twenty largest hotels in the world, was in.

▶ **Bally's:** *The fire at the original MGM Grand Hotel on November 21, 1980, which killed eighty-seven and injured 785, was the worst disaster in Nevada history. Built on that site, Bally's is known for its huge production of* Jubilee! *that features feathered and sequined showgirls and a nightly on-stage sinking of the* Titanic.

◀ **Bellagio, Fountains:** *Computers are programmed to control the fountains' 1,000 water nozzles: "oarsmen" that sway back and forth, and the "shooters" and "supershooters" that spurt water from six inches to 250 feet in the air. Over 4,000 lights and a variety of musical backdrops complete the well-choreographed enactments at the manmade lake fronting Bellagio.*

◄ **Bellagio, Chihuly Glass Sculpture:** *In keeping with its refined, artistic atmosphere, the lobby ceiling of Bellagio has been festooned with a radiant display by master glass-artist Dale Chihuly.*

▶ **Bellagio, Conservatory and Botanical Gardens:** *Just beyond the Bellagio grand lobby lies an ever-changing, impressively intricate floral compilation. Each brilliant seasonal or holiday-themed design features hundreds of vibrant, fragrant, and exotic flowers.*

◀ **Caesars Palace, Forum Shops Entrance:** *Built as an extension to the casino at Caesars Palace, when the Forum Shops opened in 1992 they comprised the first major shopping destination on the Strip. Additional levels and 175,000 more square feet in the most recent expansion extend its entrance right out to Las Vegas Boulevard.*

▼ **Caesars Palace, Forum Shops Interior:** *Billed as the most successful mall in the U.S., the Forum Shops feature the country's second circular escalator among its more than 160 stores and thirteen specialty food shops and restaurants. Nearby, throughout the day, the mythological* Fall of Atlantis *and* Festival Fountain *shows bring Roman statues to life for the entertainment of passers-by.*

▶ **Caesars Palace, Poolside:** *The 4½-acre Garden of the Gods Pool Oasis includes the Temple, Neptune, Venus, and Apollo pools, as well as a pair of whirlpools and dozens of rentable private poolside cabanas. It's not quite the Roman public baths, but the flowing fountains and classic marble statues set a calming, palatial mood.*

◀ **Paris, Eiffel Tower:**
The meticulously reproduced
fifty-story ½-scale replica of
the Eiffel Tower is not only
synonymous with Paris, Las
Vegas, but iconic to the entire
Strip. Visitors can dine at its
eleventh floor restaurant or
enjoy a guided ride up to the
top, for a panoramic view of
Vegas from 460 feet.

▲ **Paris, Arc de**
Triomphe: *The entrance to*
Paris is also defined by a
detailed ⅔-scale replica of
the famous Arc de Triomphe.
The original monument,
which proudly stands at the
western end of the Champs-
Élysées in Paris, France, was
commissioned in 1806 to
commemorate Napoleon's
victory at Austerlitz.

◀ **The Mirage:** *From dusk to midnight, the fifty-four-foot Mirage volcano "erupts" every fifteen minutes. WET Design (which also helped create the Fountains of Bellagio) reengineered the original show to be more realistic—other than the piña colada scent, which masks the smell of gas used in the fire effects.*

▲▲ **The Mirage, Tigers:** *The famous white tigers have become synonymous with The Mirage, and with the flamboyant showmen Siegfried and Roy, who introduced the exotic animals into their act. Although Siegfried and Roy no longer perform their spectacular show, visitors can still see the white tigers at the Mirage.*

▲ **The Mirage, Dolphins:** *The Dolphin Habitat at The Mirage is home to a family of Atlantic bottlenose dolphins. Next to that habitat is Siegfried and Roy's Secret Garden, which, in addition to the famous white tigers, houses golden tigers, white lions, black panthers, a snow leopard, and a four-ton elephant.*

▲ **Central Strip, Billboards:** Selling out performances of her high-ticket musical, dancing, and special effects extravaganza, A New Day, propelled Céline Dion high into Billboard Magazine's Money Makers list. Just down the street on a billboard, popular singer-comedian-impressionist Danny Gans dominates the largest free standing marquee in the world.

▶ **Flamingo Hilton:** Benjamin "Bugsy" Siegel dubbed his famous hotel-casino "The Pink Flamingo," after a playful pet name for his girlfriend, Virginia Hill. After struggling in its first few months, the resort re-opened as "The Fabulous Flamingo" in March 1947. In the early seventies, Baron Hilton acquired the property and changed its name to the Flamingo Hilton.

▲ **Treasure Island, Tangerine Nightclub:**

The trendy Tangerine Lounge and Nightclub at Treasure Island features an indoor lounge and an outdoor deck overlooking Sirens' Cove. A DJ spins rock and dance grooves, with live musical interludes by a saxophone, percussion, and stand-up bass trio, highlighted by energetic 1920s-style burlesque performances on the bar.

▶ **Treasure Island, Sirens:** *Treasure Island, now known as "TI," features a sexy, musically revamped version of their popular free outdoor show. Weather permitting, the scantily clad female Sirens lure an outdoor audience into their cove on the Strip to watch and hear the high seas pyrotechnic drama unfold four times a night.*

◀ **Venetian, Grand Canal Shoppes:** *Cobblestone walkways line the refined 500,000-square-foot shopping and dining center on the Venetian's indoor Grand Canal. Along the way to St. Mark's Square, singers, actors, and living statues perform for passers-by in the timeless, artificial, yet undeniably impressive atmosphere.*

▲ **Venetian, Lobby Ceiling:** *In May 1999, owner Sheldon Adelson opened the luxurious $1.8 billion Italian-themed Venetian Hotel and Resort with, at the time, the largest standard rooms on the Strip. Guests checking in are surrounded by opulence exuded by the ornate, lavishly decorated ceiling in the main lobby.*

▶ **Venetian, Grand Canal:** *Gondoliers sing as they guide their vessels along a quarter-mile replica of the Grand Canal in Venice, much to the delight of couples seeking a romantic respite from the casino—which hustles and bustles directly below the 280,000-gallon water feature.*

▲ **Harrah's:** *From a single small bingo parlor operated by William F. Harrah in Reno in 1937 has grown a chain of eighteen carnival party-themed casinos in the U.S. Along the way, gaming conglomerate Harrah's Entertainment has also acquired several other well-known casino brands, and now comprises the largest entertainment company in the world.*

▶ **Imperial Palace:** *The Asian-themed hotel-casino is known for its "dealertainers" (blackjack dealers impersonating celebrities) and multimillion dollar collection of automobiles (all for sale).*

Southern Strip

On December 14, 1993, the Flamingo bulldozed the last of its original buildings, including the celebrated suite in which mobster Benny Siegel once lived. Four days later, the MGM Grand opened. Between the Luxor—which had opened in October—and MGM Grand, the southern end of the Strip had added almost 10,000 hotel rooms to its growing inventory within two months.

Three years earlier, the enormous 4,000-room Excalibur (just north of Luxor) had set the tone for the decade: large-scale properties and family-driven fun. Instead of selling sex appeal, Vegas now offered video arcades, court jesters, and puppet shows. Other resorts built swimming pools by the acre, miles of rollercoaster tracks, and over-the-top theme parks.

When the giant gold-paneled Mandalay Bay opened in March 1999, it redefined the southern tip of the Strip and bridged the gap for resorts entering the modern era. Mandalay not only offered some of the same family appeal, with its eleven-acre outdoor Mandalay Beach area and immensely popular indoor Shark Reef attraction, but also dished out hip nightlife options, such as Rum Jungle and House of Blues. Furthermore, it catered to the needs of high-end clientele, first with its Four Seasons Hotel (incorporated atop the original structure) and later

with THEhotel, an additional forty-three-story tower with over 1,100 of the largest standard rooms on the Strip.

Two key pieces completed Mandalay Bay as a twenty-first century Las Vegas resort. First, nearly a million square feet of flexible meeting space made it the largest convention space on the Strip and fifth largest in all the United States. The space includes the country's largest unobstructed ballroom (without pillars), at 100,000 square feet. And second, Mandalay Place is lined with dozens of interesting shops along an enclosure that serves as not only an indoor mall, but also a comfortable walking passage to Luxor.

The next evolution in Las Vegas development is evident in the seven billion dollar Project CityCenter, planned right in the heart of the Strip, just north of Monte Carlo and south of Bellagio. The ambitious urban sprawl is conceived as a combination of over two million square feet of residential space; a 4,000-room luxury hotel-casino; two 400-room non-gaming boutique hotels; and almost half a million square feet of retail, dining, and entertainment space. This new hybrid destination demonstrates the contemporary shift in focus away from mere casinos with hotels for tourists, to more holistic, permanent-minded residential destination properties.

▶ **"Welcome to Fabulous Las Vegas":** *Commercial artist Betty Willis designed the now-ubiquitous icon in 1959, at the insistence of local salesman Ted Rogich, whose Western Neon company would build the sign. Clark County, Nevada, paid Willis $4,000 and placed the twenty-five-foot tall sign just south of the ever-growing Strip and several miles from the actual Las Vegas city limits.*

◀ **The Palms, View of the Southern Strip:** *This nighttime view from Ghost Bar, perched high atop the Palms Casino, peers across Interstate 15 at the immense properties of the Southern Strip. All four hotels—Monte Carlo, Excalibur, Luxor, and Mandalay Bay—are among the fifteen biggest in the world, with a combined total offering of over 15,000 rooms.*

◄ **Mandalay Bay, Wine Tower:** *The centerpiece of the Mandalay Bay's Aureole restaurant is this four-story wine rack. In order to retrieve bottles above head height, waiters are hoisted up the tower on special harnesses.*

▶ **Mandalay Bay, Shark Reef:** *An incredible feat of engineering and a perennial favorite with adults and children alike, Mandalay Bay's Shark Reef features more than 1,200 different aquatic species. From rare freshwater creatures, such as golden crocodiles and Amazon piranha, to various ocean denizens, including several species of shark. Shark Reef also has a pool, which is home to harmless creatures, such as rays and Port Jackson sharks, that children can pet.*

▶ **Little Church of the West:** *This freestanding miniaturized replica of an Old West mining town church is the oldest existing structure on The Strip. The thousands married here since 1942 include Betty Grable (their first celebrity), Heather Thomas, Jonathan Davis, Richard Gere and Cindy Crawford, and Elvis Presley and Ann Margaret (in the movie Viva Las Vegas).*

◀ **Excalibur, Interior:** *An Arthurian theme permeates much of this resort, with its Steakhouse at Camelot, Tournament of Kings simulated jousting show, and medieval-style weddings at the Canterbury Chapel. However Excalibur also offers an interesting variety of entertainment for both kids (a video arcade and carnival midway) and adults (the Thunder from Down Under male revue).*

▲ **Excalibur:** *When its colorful, oversized castle turrets and two massive twenty-eight-story towers went up in June 1990, Excalibur, with over 4,000 rooms, was the largest hotel in the world. Vegas has come a long way since the early nineties, but while Excalibur may not now have the glamor of the newer hotel-casinos, it more than makes up for it with its sense of fun.*

▶ **MGM Grand, Lion:** *This majestic MGM lion—the largest bronze sculpture in the United States—is perched atop a pedestal at the northeast corner of the intersection of Tropicana and Las Vegas Boulevards. Since that intersection has the most hotel rooms of any in the world, in 1994, Vegas' first elevated pedestrian walkway was installed connecting its four corners.*

◀ **MGM Grand, Pool Complex:** *As befits one of the world's largest hotels, the 6.6-acre pool complex of the MGM Grand is an amazing experience in itself. It features five swimming pools, three large whirlpools, a relaxing river, lush tropical landscaping, bridges, fountains, and waterfalls.*

▶ **MGM Grand, Studio 54:** *Acrobats, live dancers, and bungee jumpers add to the eclectic spectacle at this modern version of the notorious seventies New York discothèque. To complete the vibe, balloons and glitter often rain down on clubbers getting their groove on at any of Studio 54's four dance floors.*

◀ **Luxor:** *Since its October 1993 opening, the distinctive pyramid-shaped property that forever changed the Vegas landscape has been a nightly beacon, topped as it is by the most powerful beam of light in the world. Thirty-nine Xenon lamps combine to create a forty-billion candlepower beam, one of only two manmade phenomena—the other being the Great Wall of China—visible from space.*

▲ **Luxor, Interior:** *Guests reach their rooms, situated on the outer walls of the pyramid, by way of an "inclinator" (versus the merely vertical elevator) which travels along the inner surface at a thirty-nine-degree angle. This unique room orientation creates an inner atrium that is a vast twenty-nine million cubic feet, the largest in the world.*

▷ **Monte Carlo, Pub and Brewery:** *Monte Carlo Pub and Brewery was not only the first brewpub in a mega-resort on the Strip, but also remains one of the biggest in the nation. Predictably, many of the on-site brews have casino-oriented names, such as Winner's Wheat, High Roller Red, Silver State Stout, and Jackpot Pale.*

▲ **New York–New York, Nine Fine Irishmen Pub:** *Inspired by the adventures of nine mid-nineteenth century Irish nationalists, the pub features a grand Victorian-style bar entirely crafted in Ireland by local tradesmen. A team of nine Irish chefs create signature dishes, to be enjoyed on either patio level or indoors among traditional Irish singing, dancing, and storytelling.*

▶ **New York–New York:** *Opening in January 1997, the New York-New York casino resort boasts a 150-foot version of the Statue of Liberty, a 300-foot Brooklyn Bridge and many of Manhattan's signature skyscrapers including the Empire State Building, the Chrysler Building, the AT&T Building and the Century Building. On a clear day visitors can see Paris from Brooklyn Bridge.*

▶▶ **New York–New York:** *While the skyline within a skyline is mainly defined by familiar Big Apple landmarks, the popular New York–New York rollercoaster steals the scene. With cars painted to resemble traditional checker cabs, the Manhattan Express features a 144-foot drop and speeds up to 67 miles per hour.*

◄▲ Vegas-ized Chain Restaurants: *Signage is a big part of what makes Vegas the spectacle it is. Popular chains of restaurants, drug stores, and seemingly commonplace businesses are not exempt. The excessively flashy and over-the-top signs of these burger joints appear on the 3900 and 3700 blocks of Las Vegas Boulevard South, respectively.*

East of the Strip

In 1990, the Las Vegas Convention and Visitors Authority demolished its trademark silver dome. That same year, the LVCVA purchased the neighboring 500-room Landmark Hotel for implosion. Both moves were to make room for the expansion of the Convention Center, to encourage and support the thriving conference and trade show business in Las Vegas. Now up to 1.9 million square feet of potential exhibit area, the Las Vegas Convention Center is far from being the only meeting and event space in town.

Over a hundred properties around Vegas have from 500 square feet (smaller hotels) up to 1.8 million square feet (the Sands Expo and Venetian Congress Center) of dedicated meeting space. It has practically become a property prerequisite. In grand sum, the city's nine million square feet of convention and meeting space annually support over 20,000 meetings and conferences ranging in size from fifty to 150,000 people, adding up to seven million total conference goers. According to the LVCVA, those conventioneers generate around eight billion dollars a year in non-gaming revenue (from lodging, dining, shows, etc.), more than all the forty-plus million Vegas visitors combined contribute each year by gambling.

However folks decide to spend their money in Las Vegas, first they have to get there. Most arrive by way of Las Vegas' McCarran airport, named after Nevada Senator Pat McCarran in 1948. Currently one of the world's ten busiest airports, the facility handles over 1,000 flights a day, including non-stop services to and from cities as far away as Tokyo, Japan, and Seoul, South Korea. Fortunately for passengers, the Strip and all Las Vegas has to offer starts just a mile away.

One of the big up-and-coming areas of Las Vegas is the "Harmon Corridor." The Hard Rock Hotel and Casino was the first upscale property to set itself apart from the Strip on the perpendicular Harmon Avenue, which now comprises several multi-billion dollar projects. Actor-director George Clooney and nightclub developer Rande Gerber have signed on to invest in the three-billion-dollar Las Ramblas project, scheduled to open in 2008 with a casino, hotel, spa, condos, dining, and shopping. That same year, the stylish W Hotels Worldwide—in partnership with Edge Resorts—will open the $1.7 billion W Las Vegas, with a casino, spa, nightclubs, 300,000 square feet of meeting space, and about 3,000 combined hotel and residential units. These mixed-life urban developments represent the modern maturity of Las Vegas enterprise.

▶ **The Beach:** *Looking to distance itself from the city's dizzying revolving door of trendy clubs and lounges, The Beach bills itself simply as "A Place to Party." More than just drinking and dancing, the beer bong races, body shots, and bikini-clad staff create a "spring break atmosphere" every day of the year.*

◀ **Hard Rock Hotel and Casino:** *In 1995, when other resorts were rushing to be more kid-friendly, the Hard Rock splashed onto the scene with a cool, hip style that instantly attracted a younger adult crowd. Its rock 'n' roll attitude particularly resonates at The Joint, its intimate-but-big-name concert venue, and its notorious Sunday morning "Rehab" session at the trendy pool.*

▲ **Lotus of Siam:** *Just a few minutes down East Sahara Boulevard, Lotus of Siam prepares what has often been rated the best Thai food in the country. It is located within a modest-looking strip mall that also houses a Korean barbecue joint and Filipino karaoke bar.*

▶ **Stallion Mountain Country Club:** *Six miles down Tropicana Avenue, at the base of Sunrise Mountain, this private community boasts one of the most challenging championship golf courses in Las Vegas. Players can practice on the chipping green, deep sand bunker, expansive range, and two large practice greens before hitting the water and bunker-filled links.*

 **Las Vegas Monorail:** *Opened in July 2004, the city's mass transit monorail system allows passengers to ride from the MGM Grand to Sahara (with several stops along the Strip) in about fourteen minutes.*

 **Star Trek: The Experience:** *Almost thirty years after Elvis Presley first played at the International Hotel (now the Las Vegas Hilton), Star Trek: The Experience opened in 1998. The science-fiction theme attraction includes a "historical" museum, interactive thrill-ride, bar, and restaurant dedicated to the Star Trek universe's cult-like following.*

◄ **Atomic Testing Museum:** *The museum, on East Flamingo Road, educates the public about the more than 100 atmospheric atomic bombs detonated at the Nevada Test Site, which started in 1951 and became a popular tourist attraction (despite the dangerous fallout radiation). Although the explosions were moved underground in 1963, the testing continued until 1992.*

Please Refrain from
Touching the Artifacts
Thank You

◀ **Liberace Museum:**
Founded in April 1979 by the legendary entertainer himself, the museum features a dazzling array of the over-the-top costumes, pianos, jewelry, and cars that made "Mr. Showmanship" unique. Appointments are available to view personal mementos and memorabilia, and the store and café are open to the public.

▲ **Thomas & Mack Center:** *Prominent local bankers E. Parry Thomas and Jerome Mack established the original land foundation and feasibility studies for this thirty million dollar multipurpose facility on the University of Nevada, Las Vegas campus. Since opening in 1983, it has hosted many major concerts and become home to the UNLV Runnin' Rebels and annual National Finals Rodeo.*

West of the Strip

In the early 1900s, Downtown had Block 16, notorious for its saloons, gambling halls, and bawdy houses. Presently, Industrial Road—just east of Interstate 15—provides a close contemporary counterpart. Since prostitution is illegal in Nevada cities with populations greater than 400,000, Industrial Road is instead dotted by "costume shops," wherein couples and individuals can purchase various adult goods for private use. There are also a number of strip joints in this seedier part of town. Cab drivers around Vegas often enthusiastically promote them—solicited or not—because they get a commission for every paying customer they bring.

Across the freeway are two very popular casinos. The Rio came first, in 1990, and was distinct for its all-suite approach and enormous buffets. The Rio also features Masquerade Village, a casino and restaurant area periodically visited by the Masquerade Show in the Sky—an aerial Mardi Gras-like parade of floats suspended from the ceiling.

Across the street in late 2001, Palms Casino-Resort, owned by the Maloof family, burst onto the scene. It redefined cool for the young Hollywood crowd, the way the Hard Rock Hotel and Casino did in the nineties. In 2003, The Palms gained notoriety by hosting MTV's "Real World Las Vegas." But The Palms is best known for having its own recording studio, plus some of the hippest lounges (Rain and Ghostbar), and some of the most indulgent suites in town. Its 347-room Fantasy Tower houses the Hardwood Suite (with a basketball court, apropos since the Maloofs own the Sacramento Kings) and Hugh Hefner Sky Villa (building on the Playboy® brand). Additionally, its new fifty-story condominium hotel and spa, Palms Place, features fully furnished units ranging from 600 to 7,000 square feet.

Further west and a little north, the strangest thing of all happens in Las Vegas: it gets suburban. Beneath the beautiful looming mountains, the civilized Summerlin community is filled with shopping plazas, libraries, schools, recreational parks, and housing developments, though it does have a couple of local casino-resorts as well; the Rampart and Suncoast. The hidden jewel here is the calming sanctuary of Aquae Sulis spa at the JW Marriott.

▶ **Rio All-Suite Hotel and Casino:** *When it opened in January 1990, Rio was the first all-suite casino in Las Vegas, with rooms ranging in size from 600 to 13,000 square feet. With over 50,000 bottles, its Wine Cellar and Tasting Room is the world's largest publicly displayed collection of fine and rare wines.*

▲ **Interstate 15:** The I-15 freeway runs north-south through the U.S. and cuts right through Las Vegas. Motorists driving in from anywhere between San Diego and Salt Lake City use the popular highway, which parallels the Strip (just to the west) as it flows through town.

▶ **Rio, Aerial View:** Although Rio is set apart from the Strip, guests from other hotels often visit its Carnival World and Village Seafood Buffets, which are both known for being among the best in Vegas. The Rio also draws thousands by hosting events, such as the 2005 World Series of Poker, in its convention area.

◄▲ **The Palms, Suite:**
The Playpen Suite, shown in
both shots here, features an
exotic dancer pole, wet bar,
billiards table, and plasma
screen TV. Whereas the two-
level, 10,000 square foot
Hardwood Suite comes
complete with its very own
basketball court, scoreboard,
locker room, cheerleaders,
and team jerseys. Either one
is the perfect place to score.

▶ **The Palms, View of
the Strip:** The Flamingo
Road artery pulses east past
Rio and between Bellagio
and Caesars, as seen from
the groovy indoor/outdoor
Ghost Bar atop The Palms.
Needless to say, the hip
lounge not only has a hot
nightlife, but also, from fifty-
five floors up, one of the best
views of the Strip.

◀ **The Elvis-a-Rama Museum:** *Located on a street known more for adult entertainment, the Elvis-a-Rama Museum tends to be a crowd favorite. Founder Chris Davidson proudly displays over 2,000 items, the world's largest private collection of Elvis-owned memorabilia. Artifacts include the original Blue Suede Shoes, his Peacock Jumpsuit, and a 1960 Rolls Royce Silver Cloud II.*

▶ **Gold Coast Casino:** *As with the other Coast casinos owned by Boyd Gaming Corporation (Barbary Coast, The Orleans, and South Coast), Gold Coast is more a modest, locals-oriented property. It offers seventy bowling lanes, a 700-seat bingo parlor, and small poker room, in addition to the slots and table games found in most other casinos.*

◀ **Strip Clubs:** *Since the days Las Vegas was founded, it has been known as a city steeped in sex. It does draw the line with prostitution, which is illegal in Clark County, but strip joints, along Industrial Road and to the west, titillate thousands of convention goers and bachelor party attendees every year.*

▲ **The Canyons, Tournament Players Club:** *The TPC at The Canyons elegantly weaves its lush green turf throughout the rugged, natural beauty of the desert. Its sister course, TPC at Summerlin, co-hosts the annual PGA tournament event at which professional golfer Tiger Woods earned his first tour victory in 1996.*

▶ **Gold Coast Casino:** *When it opened in December 1986, Gold Coast was only the second major resort west of Interstate 15. After a 2002 renovation, Gold Coast was able to offer more parking, restaurants, and gaming. It also provides free shuttle service to its sister properties on the Strip.*

Outside Las Vegas

Just beyond the city limits of Las Vegas lies some of the most spectacular scenery the United States has to offer. The grandeur and serenity of the Nevada country is, for many, a welcome antidote to the glaring artificiality and glittering whirl of the city itself. Vast deserts with their characteristic Joshua trees, lakes, canyons, and mountains—a bounty of natural wonders lie within easy driving distance. And of course, there is also the manmade wonder that is the Hoover Dam: a breathtaking marvel of engineering completed in just four years during the Great Depression.

Perhaps the most striking aspect of the landscape is its diversity. Just forty-five miles northwest of Las Vegas, past Red Rock Canyon, lies the Toiyabe National Forest, thick with pine, aspen, and firs and presided over by the snow-capped Mount Charleston. A comparable distance to the northeast of the city is the Valley of Fire State Park, with incredible wind-eroded red sandstone rock formations. Both parks have well-maintained trails, some of which are very demanding, but which cater to hikers of all capabilities as well as offering picnic grounds at some of the most picturesque locations in the state.

To the west of the city is the well-ordered atmosphere of Boulder City, which was built to house construction workers on the Hoover Dam and did much to create today's Vegas. True to the wishes of its Christian founders, the town still does not allow gambling, a policy that in the thirties saw its inhabitants descend upon Las Vegas every payday. The great work of modern architecture that these men erected also created the great blue expanse of Lake Mead, which is now a National Recreation Area, devoted to every imaginable watersport and teeming with striped bass and trout.

Of course, the country surrounding Las Vegas is not entirely free of the Vegas influence. For those who prefer to gamble in a less frenetic environment, there are smaller, more laid-back casino/hotels, and for those with the need for speed, there is the Las Vegas Motor Speedway. The military is here too, at Nellis Airforce Base. Nevertheless, a significant part of the city's appeal, and one that is often overlooked by visitors, is its proximity to an unspoiled natural environment that is as impressive and exciting as Las Vegas itself.

▶ **Mount Charleston:** *At 11,918 feet, Mount Charleston is an impressive sight. In winter it plays host to hordes of skiers and snowboarders, while in the summer it gives welcome respite to the desert heat, offering spectacular views from the summit. Two demanding trails ascend to the peak, but the view is well worth the effort.*

▲ **Las Vegas Motor Speedway:** *With a pricetag of $200 million and comprising a 1½ mile superspeedway, 2½ mile road course, ½ mile dirt track, and an up-to-the-minute drag racing strip, the Motor Speedway complex is one of the nation's premier raceways as well as one of the newest. Such is the demand for seats that construction of new terraces and towers has barely stopped since its completion, and the speedway now has capacity for close to 150,000 spectators.*

▲▲ **Sunset Station:**

Part of the Station Casinos chain, founded in 1976, Sunset Station's sister resorts include Palace Station, Boulder Station, Texas Station, Santa Fe Station, and many other resorts. Many have an Old West theme.

▲ **Ponte Vecchia**

Replica: Even out of town the replica building continues. Not content with reproducing Paris, New York, Venice and elements of Rome, Nevada developers have borrowed from Florence's famous Ponte Vecchia bridge to create new and interesting apartments.

▲ **Buffalo Bill's Resort and Casino, Desperado:** *Another resort with an Old West feel that complements the natural desert surroundings is Buffalo Bill's. Here visitors can enjoy some state-of-the-art amusements, including the hair-raising Desperado. At 209 feet high and with a speed of 80 miles per hour, it is one of the tallest and fastest rollercoasters in the United States.*

▶ **Extra Terrestrial Highway:** *State Route 375 has a reputation for being the stretch of road most visited by aliens in the country, so in 1996 it was made official. Governor Miller unveiled the highway sign and spoke of his hope that any visiting aliens would make their first destination Las Vegas. He assured the audience that alien travellers' checks would be welcome in the city.*

◀ **Red Rock Canyon:**
*Rising from the desert floor,
the erosion-etched
escarpment of Red Rock has
been carved by natural forces
from red and yellow
sandstone. Despite its barren
appearance, springs and
shade support verdant
pockets. The canyon is served
by a visitor center at the
beginning of the popular tour
trail.*

▶ **Lake Mead**: *Seen here at sunset, Lake Mead was formed when the Colorado River, newly dammed, filled the canyons that its passage had eroded. Since then it has become a center for water sports and is fringed by marinas and camping grounds.*

◀ **Hoover Dam:** *Built between 1931 and 1935, the dam harnesses the Colorado River to power the neon lights on the Strip as well as making sure that the desert region has all the water it needs. An incredible feat of engineering— particularly so as it was built under budget and ahead of schedule.*

▶ **Ethel M. Chocolates:** *To the southwest of Las Vegas is the town of Henderson, which boasts the unique Ethel M. chocolate factory, producing exclusive gourmet chocolates. Tourists are welcome to tour the factory and sample its wares, and can also stroll around the botanical garden, seen here decorated for the holidays.*

▶ **Valley of Fire:** *Sixty miles to the northeast of Las Vegas, the Valley of Fire may seem a little remote, but the extraordinary rock formations more than make up for the drive. The area is also rich in archeological treasures of the Pueblo peoples who settled here over two thousand years ago. Their artwork can be seen at the Lost City Museum of Archaeology outside Overton. Hikes can be taken along four wilderness trails.*

Index

Map of Las Vegas

Craig Road

Craig Road

Decatur Boulevard

Simmons Street

Martin Luther King Boulevard

15

Pecos Road

Lamb Boulevard

Nellis Boulevard

Nellis Airforce Base

95

Rainbow Boulevard

Jones Boulevard

Cheyenne Avenue

Losee Road

Las Vegas Boulevard

Cheyenne Avenue

North Las Vegas Airport

Carey Avenue

N O R T H
L A S   V E G A S

Carey Avenue

Lake Mead Boulevard

Lake Mead Boulevard

Owens Avenue

Owens Avenue

⊙ **TOURNAMENT PLAYERS CLUB**
AT THE CANYONS

Washington Avenue

Washington Avenue

Bonanza Road

⊙ **AQUAE SULIS SPA**
AT JW MARRIOTT

THE FREMONT STREET EXPERIENCE
⊙ BINION'S
GOLDEN GATE ⊙⊙ NEONOPOLIS
GOLDEN NUGGET

Stewart Avenue

Alta Drive

LAS VEGAS ⊙
MARRIAGE BUREAU   **DOWNTOWN**

Charleston Boulevard

Charleston Boulevard

W I N C H E S T E R

Durango Drive

Sahara Avenue

STRATOSPHERE TOWER ⊙

SHOPPING PLAZA AT 953 EAST SAHARA AVE

Fremont St.

Nellis Boulevard

SAHARA ⊙
TURNBERRY PLACE
CIRCUS CIRCUS ⊙⊙ LAS VEGAS HILTON
WESTWARD HO ⊙⊙ RIVIERA
STARDUST ⊙⊙ THE BEACH
PIERO'S RESTAURANT

Sahara Avenue

SUMMERLIN

Fort Apache Road

Desert Inn Road

NEW FRONTIER

LAS VEGAS CONVENTION CENTER
Desert Inn Road

THE ELVIS-A-RAMA EXPERIENCE ⊙
⊙ WYNN LAS VEGAS
TREASURE ISLAND ⊙⊙ VENETIAN
FASHION SHOW MALL   MIRAGE ⊙⊙ HARRAH'S
RIO ⊙   ⊙ IMPERIAL PALACE
GOLD COAST ⊙   CAESARS ⊙ FLAMINGO
PALACE
THE PALMS ⊙   ⊙ BARBARY COAST
BELLAGIO ⊙⊙ BALLY'S
MONTE CARLO ⊙⊙ PARIS

Buffalo Drive

Flamingo Road

Maryland Pkwy.

Eastern Avenue

Flamingo Road

STALLION MOUNT
COUNTRY CLUB ⊙

SAM'S TOWN ⊙

⊙ ATOMIC TESTING MUSEUM
⊙ HARD RECK CASINO

515

Boulder Highway

NEW YORK NEW YORK ⊙
EXCALIBUR ⊙⊙ MGM GRAND
LUXOR ⊙   ⊙ TROPICANA
MANDALAY BAY ⊙   RESORT

⊙ THOMAS & MACK CENTER
⊙ LIBERACE MUSEUM
Tropicana Avenue

Tropicana Avenue

SPRING
VALLEY

Rainbow Boulevard

Jones Boulevard

Decatur Boulevard

Las Vegas Boulevard

Paradise Road

PARADISE
VALLEY

Russell Road

Pecos Road

Sandhill Road

to Hoover Dam ➤

McCarran
International
Airport

Sunset Road

215

Warm Springs Road

15

215

Bermuda Road

Robindale Road

N

0 ————— 2 km

0 ————— 2 miles